T0061928

SPILLING THE LIGHT

REV. JULIÁN JAMAICA SOTO

SKINNER HOUSE BOOKS

BOSTON

www.skinnerhouse.org

Printed in the United States

Revised Edition

Author photo by Leila Wice
Cover design by Kathryn Sky-Peck
Text design by Suzanne Morgan

print ISBN: 978-1-55896-918-6
eBook ISBN: 978-1-55896-919-3

6 5 4 3 2 1
28 27 26 25 24

This book is for the people who try, the people who love, the people who tell the truth, the creators of access and inclusion, and all the people with colorful hair. I love you so very much.

On all the days that end in -y.

Julián Jamaica

CONTENTS

One of the things I love most is connecting with people, both like me and different from me, in community. As I wrote *Spilling the Light,* it mattered a lot to me to imagine communities being loved, supported, and urged toward the best possible versions of themselves. As you encounter my poems, I hope my words will connect you with encouragement and care.

My poems are strongly inflected with my chosen faith, Unitarian Universalism. Unitarian Universalism is all about people of different beliefs and traditions building community together and keeping justice at the center of many of their actions and choices. What excited me was that it made room for many of the ideas that are important to me, such as accountability, compassion, and action as an expression of my values.

As I continued to grow, I learned more about what it means to take those values and make them real in the world. *Spilling the Light* came at a time when it was really important for me to express them in writing. It was also important for me to support the work that I found so important of coming together, of growing in moral and ethical strength and creating justice wherever and whenever possible.

Thank you for, as the saying goes, "picking up what I am putting down." I would be humbled and honored for my words to be in your bookbags, your pockets, your places of honor, and ultimately, your hearts. I hope to be of help on your journey.

Kind regards,
Rev. Julián Jamaica Soto

Some people are used to keeping rules; don't cross
the street when the light is red, only sensible. It turns
out that keeping rules isn't the same as keeping covenant,
which asks us, instead of keeping a bright line, to keep our
promises.

To what have we promised ourselves? To this
moment in time and place. To this community and even,
tenderly interconnected, this planet.
We promise ourselves to the idea that we
are each and all human beings. We promise that there
is something moving between us that we cannot tame
and cannot measure. The chalice is a reminder
that what flame we keep inside us cannot light the way.

The light must spill to shine.

The thing you must be is yourself.
Unadulterated, shedding the willingness
to journey alone, as though you are made of something
hard and unforgivable. You are human. You belong,
right here, right now. And together, we will chase away
the sickness, the secrets, and leave only the open
Possibility that the future is a space for growth.

—*Spilling the light*

My prayers for these stressful days
Have become sharpened. Unadorned.
A single word to the bereaved and
Wailing Mother God—mercy. Two words to
The infant child God, on trial in an unjust system—
Tender love. And for the God who is not a
White, robed, bearded father, but a migrant laborer
Daddy, with a red baseball cap, who only cries
When he thinks no one can see, not a word, but
A silent squeeze of his calloused hand to telegraph
Reconciliation, wholeness. There was a time when
More words brought comfort, but now my heart
Wants most to be true. Ready for resistance by
Unapologetic clarity and fueled by moving toward
A future in which we have made all of us free.

—*Holy Quiet*

let a powerful wind blow.
let it stoke the holy fire
that burns inside your chest.

and you must be the one
to sweep the hearth, to gather
ash. you must make room for
the flame to rise.

take away the sodden mass
of lacking care, of casual
exclusion, casual ableism.

let a powerful wind blow,
let it stoke the holy fire.

Let the light fall across your
beloved face. the same one
that sometimes makes mistakes.

let it show you more.

a way forward and together,
songs of dignity, refrains of peace.

can these bones live?

they rise, they live,
they dance.

we cannot live as less.

let a powerful wind blow,
let it stoke the holy fire.

this is how our hearts
do burn.

Brother Langston
told the truth
And boldly
set it free,
when he said

(It never was
America to me.)

Take the knife edge
out of the
parentheses.

This cannot be
enough
America for me.

—*This cannot be enough America for me*

i have tried to write this three times,
i think, supposing that one of these
mental drafts is the right one, but
the thing about a poem is that it
will either exist as the word that you
almost remember for fifteen minutes
or the stupid bass guitar riff
that will not leave your head until
you satisfy the brash demands
of a minor and annoying god.

when your friend is in grief, and
let's be real, that's today, please
do not imagine looking on the
bright side, it will be like the thing you know not to do—
look directly
into the sun, because in grief, the
light of the past is garish and the future does not yet shine.

think small in terms of cups of cocoa,
and hoodies and soft socks. imagine
that the words you say, of hope, are as
though you are shouting them through
a tunnel that goes for miles of darkness.
they will get there, but it will not be today.

less platitude, more wondering, less
positivity and more acknowledgment that grief leaves a
negative space where
something used to be.

—*i have tried to write this three times*

Last year the *it* toy was
some kind of beeping computerized
egg. The frenzy and desperation reaching
for the perfect gift. Sold out everywhere, this
egg.

Hope can be kind of like that. People
strain and struggle for the perfect definition.
Is it now? Or future perfect, as in,
we will have survived. They argue
over whether we even need a hope
more present than a *maybe*
even when you don't feel it.

A healthy hope is
the power, and beyond that the choosing to stay.
Stay with the doubt and fear.
Stay with the work that it takes to resist.
Leave giving up for another day. You
could wrestle the words or sensation of hope
to the mat. Or you could let this moment be
enough, belonging here together be sufficient.
Feast on our irrepressible power to stay.

—*A Simple Hope*

Each time people of courageous heart gather
to celebrate tradition, engage possibilities,

and explore what it means to live a life of
courage and integrity.

We offer you an imperfect welcome.

We may forget your name. We ask again
because we really want to know.

We offer hello and restroom's over there, with
hopes that you will be more comfortable.

We have a lot to share and we are glad
that you are here, bringing your own

Tradition, possibilities, courage and integrity.

We offer you a

meaningful
responsible

search for truthy; together.

We offer you an imperfect welcome—

and we want that welcome to grow
In skill and scope.

We are really glad you're here.

—*We offer you an imperfect welcome*

How do we spring back into shape?
After a long week. An election season that drags.
A broken heart that's still not healed. Raw,
but beating. No duct tape will cover those cracks.
No glue will mend the gap. Some people think
they can shame you, make you small by calling you
a snowflake. What they don't know is this:
the snow is bright because the lines and lacy edges, the
    crystals stacked, reflect back
the light shone down on them. And the light keeps
shining, just as you do. In this community, you choose
each other. You insist on blazing brilliant. Your
unique configuration is the Universe's expression
of what it means to be alive. And together, many
snowflakes make a mountain. You return to knowing
yourself and being yourself by the clarity of that
reflection. You can lay your burdens down and rest.
Lean into the place where you belong. Allow the
    brightness
of who you are, both individual and community,
to light the way toward the future
you are building with your love.

—*Snowflakes: A Guide*

Even though they are edible, someone
decided that dandelions are weeds, stragglers
to destroy, to uproot. But dandelions
never got the memo, never
thought to care. Busy instead
with dropping roots, flinging seeds, unfurling
shoots. And persistent in digging in that
taproot to depths of two or three average
adults end to end, the tiny yellow flower
survives.

You are no less resilient, reaching
both down to the strength that holds you,
and up, up to the light, out with your beauty.
And you know, having sunk your effort into
the cool, damp earth—that while dandelions
can be clipped and fought, uninvested
in anyone's opinion they throw their
sparkling futures onto the wind, tomorrow tucked
into seeds, and grow all the way back, strong and bowing
at the very same time.

—*Taraxacum*

Let my life be forward-reaching, across
the span of generations, beyond my spare

threescore and ten, let the love that I have given
be the fertile ground for what may come.

It turns out that even in the hottest, driest places in
the world—the roots remain.

Alive. Stumps nearly covered, but waiting.
Dormant seeds still containers of life.

All they are awaiting is a yes. Let my life be
the broad yes that gives new futures space to

Grow. Let the actions that I take with courage clear
away the damage, unearth the tender roots and

Bright green leaves turned toward the sun, that
living core, still growing, greening heart.

They remind us that even this struggling,
overheated Earth has the power to

Regenerate. So may I, may we, love others even
when conditions are tense, make justice when

The situation seems beyond remedy, the breaks
beyond repair and tend the beauty, the living root.

—*Let my life be forward-reaching*

We haven't found enough dreams.
We haven't dreamed enough.
—Georgia O'Keeffe

The world makes many demands on
your time, your skin, your heart. Until
you are left gasping and wondering
if you will ever do enough,
have enough, be enough. Stop your
counting, measuring, and checking.
You are enough. So much more than
enough, made from fragments
of the galaxy.

You
do
measure up.

And to recover from
the doubt pressed upon you,
the antidote for doubt is dreaming.
All the dreams that call to you,
lime green and frosting pink dreams.
The other soft and tender dreams
that run blue to gray,
sky indistinguishable from lulling
sea. The dreams that seem impossible—
listen: that's their nature. If they
had already happened, then they

would be realities, solid and smooth,
like the round bone home of an
unbroken egg. Be brave enough
to name your dream. Nurture it. And
allow the rhythm of your breath
to bring your dreams to life.

—*Finding Our Dreams*

This is what I shall tell my heart,
and so recover hope.
—Lamentations 3:21

Shall we speak life
into each other's hearts?
Remembering. Returning
to the futures we are building, the infinite
dimensions of growth
we are committed to.
A touchstone of loving kindness
can be our starting place,
Unyielding cornerstone.

This is what I
shall tell my heart,
that this community
is, at its best, a source
of unrelenting kindness
and that when the world
is broken, on fire, at war,
forgetting its humanity,
we are here to say it back:
each beloved, all belong,
not as a platitude,
but as a way of living,
a choice in being.

This is what we shall
tell our hearts, that to be
alive is to hold, tender
as a sprouting plant,
one more chance to try again,
stubborn yes,
as plain to notice as all
the ways that we have,
before this moment,
been unwilling to risk
or to imagine that
things could be
different than they
are now.

Let us say, to our hearts
that are scarred and sometimes
weary, that they can lead the way.
We are prepared to follow;
And on the path forward,
we may find our endurance
tested, but in the end discover
that the consequence of action—
natural, logical, magical—
is a perennial specimen
of hope.

—*Let us say to our hearts*

This is a charm for hope. The first thing
to do is tie a string around your finger.
Remember that you are not alone. Think
of the ways that our best shared futures
are braided inextricably with your own
present and your destiny. The second thing
is to untie the string and let the knots
and tightness fall away. Let the burden
of bleakness roll off your sore shoulders.
Resistance on these opaque horizons
only requires one source of strength, one
ray of light. Remember that persistence
doesn't require all the answers up front. Only one.
Fortunately for all of us, we have one response:
to remain together through awkward times
and happy ones. We remember
and we find our resolve in one another.

—*A Charm for Hope: A String*

part 1

being universalist is like
a person who went
on a long journey.

people think it is
a great movement
of emotion that causes

the idea that G-d
would never
abandon their
own nature.

but it is just as much
a finely wrought work of
mathematics
(stay with me—it is a
long journey)

part 2

here's the thing: of all the
7.93 billion people in
the world, it seems unlikely,
bordering on improbable,

that yoooouuu (play
this note tenderly, as
for a sibling—on a kazoo)
are the only imperfect one.

I think God knows, or at
least suspects, that our
hearts are that tough, but
also that tender and some
times they heal up like

super glue on ceramic—
definitely back together,
chipped, glue showing,
crooked, and ready to be
used.

It seems implausible that
not only are the rest of us
stardust (and you are not
made of less) but the
rest of us are

in development:

egg to tadpole to frog
crumb to sponge to bread
mote of dust to
expanding star.

part 3

being universalist is
also this: that not
disposing of people

means that we see them—

what materials do they use
to make amends?

(an apology of words
An atonement of actions)

take their second chance
and maybe a third and even
more, because

if humans live threescore
years and 10, that's 70,
that leads me to believe

that you may make
more than a single mistake.

When I apologize for this,
it is with the calm
understanding
that this is one of
the harder parts
of being human.

If I laugh, it is only
recognition and sympathy,
supposing that in your
complicated quantum
meat state.

part 4

you will encounter a

kaleidoscope, a ball pit,
of the ridiculous and the
absurd, as a secretary bird
or a flashlight fish, but also
dizzying heights of compassion

and the humble, pockets turned
out, palms up, clear-eyed
non-defensive posture

mudra of ultimate despair

In the end, all will be well:
you are beloved and
you belong.

here. In this place.
now. In this time.

Imperfect and longing.

Forevermore.

being universalist is like
a person who went
on a long journey.

in the name of
the future, her children
and all we may yet imagine:

amen.

—*being universalist is like*

Some people, maybe you—hold up—
because I'm not mad like that, and
we really should talk this out.
Some people want to know why we have to
use the word "white" and the word "supremacy"
together.

And I will tell you one story of why, but first
you must imagine that the skin of the poet being brown
cannot change the nature of the alphabet.

That emotional intelligence requires that we notice
who we're willing to watch,
unable to survive.

The reason those two words (white + supremacy)
matter is that they describe with photorealistic clarity—
and remember, that a photo of a thing is not actually
the thing—the pattern that it's
easiest not to notice.

The pattern, hewn granite default in which person
is short for "white person."
And civil rights are code for—
the "rights of straight, white
able-bodied cis folk."

The fact that you mean something different
is a beautiful beginning, but to heal that
dehumanization of Black folks, of people of color,
you can make the choice to

Call the wounding something honest.
Having centered white folks for lifespans
end to end, we can shift to explicit naming
that each and every life is important,
not just the ones that belong to white folks.

—*But Why This, Why Now*

I know that you are hungry for justice
and sometimes when you fail, it feels
like the times when you open
the refrigerator door, look inside and close it,
nothing having met your appetite.
But there is always trying again.
There is the fact that one just act is
the beginning. And together we can build
another. The gnawing hunger for a different
future is one that we feed in the present.
Your diligence, your tenacity, your
willingness to learn, not just know,
but also do, hunger shaping how you
nourish, feeding one another
with the long spoons of your compassion,
until you're strong enough to feed the part
of the world that you can reach.

—*Blessed Are the Hungry*

On these days, am I meant to call up courage?
Depending on what day it is, that might not work.

Are you extending me a hand? King Solomon said
that with a friend you can face the worst. Helpful

because sometimes the world is too much (and too
much with us.) And between the fires and floods,

the fascists and the fools, sometimes my courage,
beset by grief and disappointment, fails. This is

the truth. But it is still possible to act, fear present,
courage small, to seed the futures we believe in.

Stay. Connected to and for one another. Hold fast
to the mission that we share. There is no shame in

being afraid; fear also wants to live. But if we seek
the fuel for bravery we take from one another and

from the tiny space between contractions of our,
against the astronomical odds, still beating hearts.

—*Am I meant to call up courage?*

you are not hard to love and respect
your existence is a blessing. your pronouns
are not a burden or a trial;
they are part of your name, just shorter.
some of our kin use only their names,
where pronouns would be,
the names they are called. remember that
someone getting them wrong is not a poor
reflection on you. it is not your fault.

your body (really and truly)
belongs to you. no one else.

the stories of your body
the names of your body's parts
your body's privacy
the sum of your body's glory.

it is not okay for anyone
to press their story of you,
back to the beginning
of your (of our) liberation.

we will find the people ready to be
on the freedom for the people way.
we will go on. no one can rename you
Other, it can't stick, as you offer the gift
of being and saying who you are.

mostly, though, your stories belong to you.
your joy and complexity are beautiful,

however you may choose to tell it (or not
tell it). some folks (cis) may take their liberty
for an unholy license. you are beloved. please
keep to our shared tasks of
healing
getting free.

—dear trans*, non-binary, genderqueer
and gender-expansive friends and kin:
(and those of us whose gender is survival)

The magic of your palm is that though empty,
it can be filled. But look at it. One of the planes
of creation with which your body is equipped.
Lines sweeping out to fingers and the marvels
of opposable thumbs, that single leap toward
grasping. And do not fear if you do not have hands.
We know that you, too, create. And together, we
take up what it means to hold a value and make
it come alive. More than only thought and feeling,
rather—being, doing, and becoming. A sculpted
expression, colorful, an embodiment of

why we are,
what we do,
and what we will
yet become.

—*The Magic of an Empty Palm*

To be free, you must embrace
the breadth of your own existence
without apology, even if they try to take
it from you. You must know, not that you
can do whatever you want; you are not
a kudzu vine, eating entire hillsides for
the purpose of feeding your own lush life. You
must know instead, that inside you are entire
Universes—milky blue, magenta, and gold—
expanding. But to actually be free, you must
know and you must fight for the entire
Universes inside of everyone else.
Being free is not a license, but
A promise.

—To the people who have mistaken freedom for liberation
(with thanks to Rev. Leela Sinha)

People are not
long division problems.
Their resources almost never
divide evenly into their concerns,
which is how we end up with
remainders of fear and anger,
and such tentative beauty, having
only recently been liberated from
the imposition of thousands
of inapplicable shames. People
do not imagine being messy
and unresolved, until their broken
hearts remain unmentionable.
Eventually, point three repeating,
awkwardly at first and then
with an intonation and rhythm
meant to simulate being just fine,
[no problem!].

People are not
long division problems. You cannot,
should you, meaning well, try this,
fix or solve them. [Reminder:
they will almost never come out even.]
What you can do is be a welcome in
a wounded and suspicious world. You
can recognize the person as who

they are. You can assume that without
the gift of their humanity, even when
it is complicated, none of the sum of us
can arrive at the answer of who
we are meant to be, collective and whole.

—*Neither divisor nor dividend*

There must be fuel.
There must be a spark,
and there must be oxygen.

We have principles and ethics.
The fuel of the fire we would light.

The spark is what passes between us,
along with our aliveness, our possibility.
Spirit moving in us is our clear invitation—
embossed, addressed, sealed with wax, tied
with ribbon. The spark is a seed of fire that
must be treasured and tended that it may
bring the light.

We have passion. The air without which
nothing thrives, least of all the blaze
of covenant, justice, and kindness we would
illuminate, both with who we are and what
we do.

All of these an invitation to bring to life
the blaze of liberation that is meant to light our
way and to dispel the fog of cruelty and grief.
It brings us instead to a hearth around which
we gather to be nourished, energized, and
warmed and where we get ready to disperse,
enlivened.

—*The Spark Between*

Until you are a couple of years old,
people count your age in months.
I met a baby with blue eyes and dinosaur pajamas. Four
    months.
I couldn't stop thinking about
how much information he was collecting
and enjoying. I watched him observe
his fists with studious wonder.

Yes. Let me also

Hold up my fist and
look on it in wonder.

What can a fist, a hand, hold?
What can it let go?

Cascading through
open fingers.

Let me use my adult fist
to rise. To crush my own cruel,
insincere doubt.

Let me have a Jael fist of iron
to pound a stake into the future
we will build.

Yes, small one, yes.
The wonder of a fist.

—*The Wonder of a Fist*
(For Lucas)

Everything is still on fire. Despite
your best efforts. In addition to living,

it is clear, that fire or not, you must
level up in what it means to thrive.
Right now, that means wrestling with
the truth in the fact that everything is
not all your fault.

I am sorry that everything is still on fire.
Once hate catches, the winds of "not my
problem" blow and the blaze is hard
to stop. But hard is not impossible. Not yet
is different than never. You, in community,
have an answer. You have a response to systems
of power and control and to the cost
of suffering.

You and your community, together, are the answer.
You are not only a people of flame but also a people of
cold, clear truth. You know both where you fall short
and where you flourish, and where you
still reach.

Everything is still on fire, but all is not lost.
you remain, more nimble than steadfast. More

unshakable than swayed by the latest rage.
You are here to put out the ravenous flames and
heal the world. Enough is enough.

—*everything is still on fire*
(with thanks to Rhiannon)

I cannot prove to you that
I am a person. But you can
hold my hand, cool and dry,
while we pray, or just
breathe, ragged breaths
catching on our aching
ribs.

I cannot prove to you that
brown skin is holy, that
Black skin is sacred,
but you can know it,
luminous and irrepressible,
the tabernacle of your own
liberation.

I cannot even
prove to you that every
queer body, every trans and enby
body, every ace and bisexual body
sings back to the universe its
immense generative power of
yes.

I cannot prove to you with
quadratic certainty that what
a disabled body holds is a story
of wisdom beyond perfection,
like a red sun emerging from
behind a cloud of dust.

So the answers that I have
for a country hacking up
a death rattle, and a democracy
with a wheezing, waxy pallor
are about our courage to
love.

Our desperation, not only for survival
but also to tread above the worst
of our collective nature. and to get
each other free, unashamed that
there came a day when we were
willing to risk looking foolish
to simply stay
together and alive.

—*I cannot prove to you*
that I am/we are human.

after the grief and the loss
the women showed up bearing
a gift for their dead Friend.
that would not be repaid.
the gift I can bring to my Friend is:
showing up. when They appear
over and over, alive in the most
unlikely of ways. I can show up
and tell the story of life unlikely
in the face of no agreement.
and where death persists, life
continues undeterred. let us speak
of that. of showing up when grief is
thick on our shoulders like a wool
coat. and when there is no sign that
life, much less joy, may yet return.
because where two of us, or three,
let's say, stop to think of our Friend,
to rest in Their love, there they will,
celebrating the unlikeliest of Loves,
show up.

—*Showing up for (F)friend(s)*

Being a person of color in
America today is like
the person who stepped aside
for passing hikers at the Grand Canyon
and tripped and fell four hundred feet instead,
except that if you are a person of color,
people search for your criminal record
as you fall. They tut that, after all, you
could have been more compliant. They
include the subtext—free of charge—your
falling is a clear indication that you deserved
it. Whatever it is, whatever flavor
of dehumanizing is being served.

When you are falling
they assert that you just don't get it
because your parents were immigrants,
which is only a dirty word in the mouth of
a colonizer feigning innocence. When you
are a person of color, you are never [on]
the winning side. As you fall, they tell you
that all hikers matter and are worthy of first
aid. Never mind that you will reach the bottom
Dead.

—*Being a person of color in America today*

Bring your broken hallelujah here.
Bring the large one that is beyond
repair. Bring the small one that's
too soft to share. Bring your broken
hallelujah here. I know that people
have told you that before you can give
You have to get yourself together. They
overstated the value of perfection
by a lot. Or they forgot. You are the gift.
We all bring some broken things, songs
and dreams, and long lost hopes. But
here, together, we reach within.
As a community we begin again. And
from the pieces we will build something new.
There is work that only you can do. We
wait for you.

—*Bring your broken hallelujah here*

In this community, we hold hope close. We don't
always know what comes next, but that cannot dissuade
    us.
We don't always know just what to do, but that will not
    mean
that we are lost in the wilderness. We rely on the
    certainty
beneath, the foundation of our values and ethics. We
are the people who return to love like a North Star and
    to
the truth that we are greater together than we are alone.
Our hope does not live in some glimmer of an indistinct
    future.
Rather, we know the way to the world of which we
    dream,
and by covenant and the movement forward of one right
    action
and the next, we know that one day we will arrive at
    home.

—*We Hold Hope Close*

Isn't it a weird word, though—
prevail? How could we win before
we encounter the challenge? Before
what? Not like preheat an oven or
pre-measure an ingredient. It turns out
that the pre- doesn't mean before
in the way that we're all used to. It
comes from a Middle English p-r-a-
which means toward. Toward greater
strength. That and a quarter will
get you a gumball. Let me reassure
you.

No one knows everything, even
though some people wisecrack like
they do.

You could not know before
right now what this moment would
call for. Knowing, you now move
toward greater strength.

Knowing, this very moment you
teach yourself and your communities
what and how we shall be more able

not simply to survive the day, but also
to take the future back in your own
hard-working hands, our communal
resistance and possession.

You will prevail if you commit. Doing
the next thing because it is next. Moving
toward greater strength, building the skills
it takes to heal the aching world.

—*Prevail: an etymology*

There are a lot of ways to stay alive.
You can wear soft clothes and focus
on brushing your teeth and hydrating.
You can ask yourself what you need
and not be mad when you don't have
an answer, only a shrug. You can breathe in.
And then, with care, you can also breathe out.
Taking the thing one single breath at a time.

You can give yourself a chance. Remember
not only your mistakes, but also all the ways
that you matter. From eyelash to shoelace, you
matter. You matter when you are sad, when
the world is heavy, like wet laundry, dragging from
your arms. You matter when you are angry
and you use your teeth like welded prison bars
to keep the words that might cause harm from
escaping past your lips.

There are many ways to stay alive.

You can come, heart wrapped in
several layers of foil, mashed into a plastic
box with an ill-fitting lid, to a place where
people say your name like it is good news.

You can always fight your way toward freedom.
I recommend that you decline the option
of struggling by yourself. The point is to get
your life. There was this wise ruler

who said once that by ourselves we each are
unprotected, but two people together can
face the worst: [the failure, the heartbreak,
the upending of the worlds we hold in our
hearts, and the secret shame that we will
shed like the skin of a smooth snake, though it
will take some time.] And with three people,
you being one of them, you may find that
eventually, all will be well.

—*There are lots of ways to stay alive (ILYSM)*

Worrying is like an elephant. The more someone
tells you not to elephant, the more it becomes
real and wrinkly, tooth and trunk. And, anyway
did you even say you wanted an elephant taking
up the whole entire living room? You never do
when you are anxious. But Anxiety didn't ask,
is content instead to put muddy boots on your
velvet mental furniture. Laughing unconcerned
when you actually care. Anxiety is like a song that
gets stuck in your head, except the tune is off, and
the words keep getting messed up, but you still
can't get rid of it. The fear, the stress,
the skin-crawling dread.

Blessed are the anxious.

Sorry that it's hard,
and you're not always wrong that things sometimes
fall apart and end up worse than when we started.
Blessed are you when you try, fear gripping your arms
as though it is afraid of losing you, even though, what
you know is that it's never far away. There is so much
unseen labor in managing everything just under the
      surface.

Blessed are you, the tired ones, the ones who
bring along their elephants and still make room for what

may be possible, for joy, for love, and for a future that may, even though we can't be sure of it, be even more abundant and full of every possibility of peace.

—*The Elephant in the Room, Every Single Room*

A friend of mine told me about a friend
of hers. (Don't worry. A *lot* of good stories
start that way.) Whose mother gave them
this piece of advice: "I know they look dry,
seem dead, this forest of what was a sway
of pink and purple, with their spots and tendrils,
paper-thin beards and cheeks, these
orchids now sticks. You must save them;
put them away for a later season.

Then, as is likely to happen to people with the
Human condition, the mother died. And we both
feel and imagine the ocean of grief, the riptide of loss,
the tornado of tearing the muscle of heart that
the friend underwent, undergoes, we have undergone.
And then there was the day that the friend opened
a door; the sun shone in, leaves quivered, flowers
danced in fluid silence. Person still alive,
flowers come awake.

This is the advice. When the cute part of your
life fades and the pretty part becomes more faint in
memory—you must save what is bare and dry, a
definite black line against the gray and foggy sky.
The beauty will return if you leave a space for it.

I must urge you to this because it is likely that you or I
will have a dry time in the not so distant future and we
remain, locusts and drought notwithstanding, always
each other's harvest.

—*The Advice*

you tend to think that
the place from which you
view the world is common.

and if you are white, you are
standing higher on the slope.
i am seated in my wheelchair.

it's not that bad, you say.
and i am sliding toward the bottom.
i see a few people making it, you say.

as you look up, your back turned
to me now. i am still sliding. but
i hold on. i try to speak above the

voices that prescribe the right way
to make it; has to do with fitting in,
here at the top. we have traditions,

customs. and why are you yelling?
that is not the way we do it here,
but i can see those who have slid,

the Black, the brown, the queer and
trans, the old, have slid all the way to
the bottom of the hill, their bones, their

blood mashed into the way that you
find yourself rising, telling the white
story as the right story, over and over.

it is not that bad as you stand on their

necks, on their backs, and obliviously
eat their faces, just a few bites.

no one was using them anyway.

—*Notes on a Napkin (White Supremacy)*

If I sent you a text, it would say simply:
I have good news. Would you text me back?
If I sent you a note, on my very best notecard
with a sticker and a postage stamp, that said,
You are not going to believe this! In a way
meant to allow you to suspend some
disbelief, not tease you for being skeptical.
Would you read the inside?

You are used to casual mentions of the place
where you belong—faith, ethics, love in action,
but what if more were possible? What if you had a sign—
garish, neon, bringing with enthusiasm
the occasional blink and an ongoing bug zapper buzz?

You are the oasis. You are the hospital for
broken hearts. Whatever it is that keeps you
shy, reserved, appropriate in telling where it is
that folks can belong and grow back their injured
hearts, is worth a challenge. Grow unashamed
at your own healing and connection. Grow proud
of your diligence in keeping mutually dependent
promises. Grow affectionate and supportive toward
your community, even though it is imperfect. But
most of all, be foolish for love, tender-
hearted for love, and bold for love.

Boldly, you must hang your light. Neon,
buzzing, bright. And do not be chagrined when
your light blinks. It is a silent song of yes, you,
you are welcome here. Boldly, give your love
and arrive at your joy.

—Boldly, you must hang your light

El molcajete de mi abuelita

My grandmother's grinding
stone

se ha perdido.

has gotten lost.

Se le regaló a un pastor.

It was gifted to a pastor.

(Una vez, en su oficina, vi que
ahí era donde ponía su biblia,
en el lugar donde había maíz,
alimento fortificante.)

(Once, in his office, I saw that
that was where he rested his
Bible—the place where there
was corn, fortifying nutrition.)

Sobrevivir está hecho de las
sombras del molcajete. Está
hecho de todas las formas del
trabajo de las manos de mi
abuelita.

Surviving is made of the shad-
ows of the grinding stone. It is
made of all the forms of work
of my grandmother's hands.

El encaje. La tortilla. El
futuro de sus doce hijos, bor-
dado con cariño, pintado con
fe necia, dobladillos de miles
de oraciones.

The lace. The tortilla. The
future of her twelve chil-
dren, embroidered with love,
painted with stubborn faith,
hems of thousands of prayers.

El molcajete se perdió, pero
las mujeres, la bisabuela y
las abuelas se quedan para
siempre.

The grinding stone was lost,
but the women, the great-
grandmother and the grand-
mothers remain forever.

Ellas son mis molcajetes,
de permanencia, de cono-
cimiento, haciéndome mi
misma y mi comunidad.

They are my grinding stones,
of permanence, of knowing,
becoming both myself and my
community.

—*My grandmother's grinding stone*
El molcajete de mi abuelita

The part of clouds that is not water
are pieces so tiny that no
human eye can see them. They float
so fast and easily that weather scientists
identify them as aerosols. Don't, don't
fall asleep because I said a science thing.
I want you to remember that all around you
dust, atoms, tardigrades and other tiny things
that hold the world together are doing dances
for you. Without that tiniest of dust specks
in perfectly clean air a cloud would struggle
to ever form. Which is true of any thing
that you want to grow. It must start small.
There are people who would tell you
that this chain reaction of events is
one on which everything, for them,
rises and then falls. The smallest dust, the
cloud, the rain. Allows the earth to drink, to
grow our food, to feed an ecosystem, to fill
the rivers and lakes from which we drink.
The part that is not water is the tiniest dot
of dust. On this small and humble thing we
find that everything does rest.

—*The part that is not water*

What it means to have a pet is to
love someone who speaks a language
you do not. A dog will bow and prance,
a cat will purr and blink. A guinea pig
will giggle and squeak. A long time ago
a friend of mine had a dog with soft ears,
and considered herself the pup's guardian.
A gentle way to think of protecting
and caring for a friend, such a small gesture
of respect for a source of boundless love.
The dog's long pink tongue lolling in a goofy
grin. The cat convinced that kneading
and grooming are crucial to this day. A bird
asking for a treat, bending a wing to wave.

These are friends. They are loves. It's
kind of a surprise that you should love
someone so much who would eat the butter
on the table if they could get away with it,
and gets endless hair on the sofa when they
aren't even supposed to be on the furniture.
When they are called companion animals,
it's such an open, tender truth. The endless
cuddles and tricks and loyalty. The comfort
of fingers to fur and big, adoring eyes.
These are friends. They are loves. They
stretch our hearts and fill them with

their abundance of kindness. When they
are gone, our hearts remain larger,
though their absence leaves room
for expanses of grief. Their love
champions and companions us still.

—*When your best friend has four or so legs*

Sometimes I codes/
witch. I know you will tell me
that's not necessary. But I
have seen them when I say
howdy, smile thin smiles that
are ten percent relief and ninety
percent teeth. I can make funeral
potatoes like I was born to them.
But I was not. I have lost the words
beneath my tongue because
sinvergüenza doesn't translate.

And it takes a lot of words to say
how dare you be so filthy disrespectful
in a smooth, non-threatening kind of way
that makes no more sound than the snick
of a tissue sliding out of a box:

But I learn them. I wrap them round
my ribs because codes/
witching is not without its blows. I
make the same soft sounds over and
over, trusting they are like breezes
over dry sand. Leaving volute lines
that mark the path that we still take.

No creas que mis abuelitas no saben
cuanto crees que soy menos humana,
menos ministra. Aunque me dedique
mi animo, mi cuerpo, mis horas.
Nada que ver.

It's all good. We do what we must.
Persevere.

—*Codes/witching*

There is a moment before dawn
when the night is firmly in charge of the sky.
There is no arguing with the opacity that holds
both a fertile imagination and cover of destruction.

Just hold on.

There is the moment when the dream we share
is newly born, wet and wriggling in our hands.
Sometimes it's true that salvific futures look
vulnerable and small before us. We remain unsure.

Just hold on.

Anything good was small at first.
You know that Dr. King said, "I have a dream."
It definitely was not the I have a reality speech.
It was real in a different way that could be felt,
that could be shared.

They held on.

That dreaming speech happened in August 1963.
And you know what came before was April:
a letter from a Birmingham jail. One moment did
inform the other, but the future being built
could not be known with certitude.

They held on.

We gather, certain only of
our power to be human. Finding ourselves committed
to keeping our word and being our covenant.

And when we fail to keep our promises
we don't throw them away, labeled as impossible.
We take up our courage. We begin again.

We hold on.

Sprinkled in the wind, we can hear the question:
If we are not white supremacy shaped
into religious robes and rituals, then who are we?
We are present, both in attention and in the answer.
We are here.

We hold on.

We contain multitudes, not just of questions
and contradictions, but also of possibilities.
We continue to labor for the creation of community
in which all of us, not just each, but every part of us,
is welcome in our home of faith.

We hold on.

—*We Hold On*
(With thanks to Rev. Leslie Takahashi
and the Unitarian Universalist Association Commission
on Institutional Change)

If we are to dismantle the systems that
grind our siblings to make their bread,

we must know their names. And knowing
their names, we must call them to account.

Racism is a name that is easy to dismiss,

hiring practices a nuance much
more subtle.

White supremacy sounds so strong to
good liberal folk who mean well;

we much prefer to speak of
the way things have always been.

Executive sessions, closed doors meant to shield
sensitive matters, become a weapon for
bad behavior done in secret,

discomfort alleviated at all costs,
accountability certainly something
someone could practice.

It is a very old wisdom that asserts that if you
know the name of something—a fantastical
creature, an object, you can defeat a foe;

the bias that you have for white skin
at the not-so-hidden cost of the lives
of people of color—we call that
white supremacy.

—*The Name of Tyranny*

Where is Life sending you? Here. Now.
Don't flinch. Where will you go? Across
the street. To learn the name of your neighbor.
Across the city to support interfaith dialogue, to
witness the practice of neighbors whose faith has
different names, uses different words than yours.

Is Life calling you to come closer to the grief
around you? Not with words, but with empathy
and kind silence. Sometimes there is no fixing
sadness and we must instead weather it. But together we
make the journey much more possible than alone. Where
does life send you?

Go where your heart pulls you. Catch up to that insistent
call, to the thing that waits for you,
the soft place where your talent can rest and your joy
bubble up. The sound? The lights? The homeless shelter?

There is somewhere you can be. There might not be a
parking space reserved sign you can see, but there is a
yes for you from the Universe. Whether your task is
to work or to heal, to rest or to play, it is time to go, to
go where Life sends you and be who you are meant to be.

—*Where Life Sends You*

Our history is always with us. Across organisms,
offspring receive a maternal inheritance, DNA:
strands of instructions, twisted together
and reaching into the future. What is the secret tucked
in the folds of tiny parts of cells? How does that
legacy keep us alive? We are each and all holding
a gift of humanity, fragile, wrapped in tissue. We
are connected by those gifts, generation after
generation, failure after new attempt, dream
upon dream, creation from disaster. I know. You're
just not sure—about your place, about this time,
about what, if anything, is possible. Just try to
remember that people have built splendid new
futures from much less than the magic
and the bequest of life that you now hold.
The world is waiting for your gifts—an invitation.
Do not blame yourself for being wonderful. There is
no shame in this. You must, instead, expand,
and, understanding the destiny of your inheritance,
the here, the now, the you—you must fly.

—*Mitochondrial Gift*

When I was a child, someone told me that
if you hold a seashell to your ear, you can hear
the ocean. When I was in middle school, I learned
that what you hear is not the ocean. It's just
the blood rushing through your ears. And that's fine.
But I still wonder if a broken seashell has any
good kind of song. The song of half a wave might
be a measure of grief. The Bay of Fundy when it
is empty. The bacteria flats in Yellowstone, steaming
copper and blue, smelling of sulfur and somehow
a cradle for life. Anklets of kelp forest. Even
mostly empty, the ocean cannot help but brim
with tokens of aliveness, reminders of beauty, and
the plain, unabashed assurance that broken things—
seashells, people, and times of love—have beauty all
their own, if we can dance in the offbeat, if we can
stand a little grit with the gorgeous gifts of
this wide world.

—*Broken Shellsong*

What it takes to survive
is more than an emergency
blanket, a fire starter, and a
hatchet. It requires recognizing your
self, after someone has tried to
blur your divine image. It requires
saying your own name over and
over, but only for your own benefit
and glory. For finding your root to
the earth beneath you and sky
everywhere. For illuminating opaque
horizons when you're not sure if
you'll ever recover, ever grow.
Outliving intentional harm [one
evil] requires a single ember banked
in your wheezing, dizzy heart. And
if you find that tiny fire smothered,
smug patriarchy shrugging off the
work of stained hands and starched cuffs.
Please, friend, please do not despair; we
here share the light of our belonging with
and to one another. The work of outliving
evil cannot be completed in a single
moment. Recognize and remember who

you will yet become. We will share our
spark with you; we will say your name
with honor and know you as healing
and as free.

—*Survivor/ship*

Can we develop the skill of remembering the future?
Can we commit to build the community that will extend
into a time that we only know by memory because it
will outlast us? Memorize the compass points of the day
yet to come: the truth, the love, the fire, the endless yes
of the horizon. Shake the scales from your imagination:
Reach. Stretch. Rise. There is no more time
for pretending
that everything can be all right without your care, without
your attention. You can mourn, grief being more
real at times
than the promise of the sunrise. More real than the piece
of the moon, that by inconstant silver turns, disappears.
And yet. While we may mourn changes,
losses, deceptions,
and betrayals, beneath the ash we find the ember. We
weep and then, as we have learned from labor movements,
we organize. Remember the day toward
which we gather,
the tomorrow toward which we advance. It is with
your actions today that you engage that muscle memory,
that sense of smell, the ragged velvet feel of a day that
you have never lived. It is also your day.
Remember it well.

—*Remembering the future*

I'm not prepared to hear you say one thing, and
watch you do another, without even mentioning it.
I'm not talking about mistakes. You know we all make
those. Sometimes we speak too soon and think too little.
We worry more about procedures than promises. We
let fear and guilt keep our choices and actions small.
Those things, common and human, keep calling us forward
to different, better choices. I'm thinking of
a different thing,
in which you know the right thing to do and spend entire
notebooks of calculations on figuring out how not to do it;
or, conversely, you give it no thought at all. It's
understandable that to learn the student must be
ready. And if you choose not to be ready while
the world cries out for your help, choose to linger in
indecision and shrug off the human cost, you are
wasting the gentle flexibility of grace and as Frederick
Douglass said, "using your liberty for unholy license."
You must account for this day. Choose justice. You must
account for your gifts. Generate love. Your effort in
community is a precious resource. Take courage.
Move with urgency toward every possibility.
Please hurry. Don't stop.

—*Time for the Work*

People wake up to ordinary days all the time,
and then, somehow, as though things were just
too peaceful, they experience drastic reversals
of fortune. The car resting on its roof. The fall,
the broken bone. The less than hoped for grade,
the broken heart when a pet dies. You get it.
You never know what's in a day. Except you; you
are the golden thread running through. I know
that these reversals will test you. You may move
through, burdened with a fresh, wet grief. Or
for now, you may arrive at this moment unscathed:

What you need to know is that there is nothing larger
than the love that is your destiny. And the love may,
at times, feel opaque and distant, like a looming
thundercloud, too far to reach. If that's too hard
to locate, find your breath, a thread of your life.
Find your community, friendly face and open hand.
What's true is that some changes call for every
skill that we possess. The deeper truth remains:
changes will eventually change. Let your heart
flex. Let it grow. Allow a reversal to be a moment
in which you are the constant, while you give
yourself kindness and heaping, joyful love.

—*Reversals of Fortune*

I wish the knowledge
were easier to come by,
that individualism is
just a scam, that
you are always
the butterfly wings.
You are always
the storm.
Edward Lorenz,
a weather scientist
from MIT, is
sometimes misquoted
on this, as the premise
that the
flap of a
butterfly wing
can cause
a hurricane in a
different part
of the world.
Shorthand that isn't
all that close to
a representation
of the math-turned-
weather scientist's work.
He proposed that,
Should we make
even a tiny alteration

to nature,
we will never know what
would have happened
if we had not disturbed it,
since subsequent changes
are too complex
and entangled
to restore
a previous state.
Which is to say
that you have an
immeasurable effect
on the system. It
will change and you
will shape its DNA.
You must not believe
the lying lie that
you do not matter,
that whatever change
you can organize is
so insufficient as to
not be worth
your time,
your energy,
your life force.
You must be willing
to dream a dream
that carries forward

your community. This
is how we rise.
This day is polluted
with a mistrust of truth,
fertile and warm medium
for unchecked cruelty and
power. You must choose
to scream the truth
until every leaf and stone
bears unrepentant witness
to what happens when
you try to cage and smash,
to pin and frame a butterfly
and their thousands and thousands
of fabulous, flamboyant friends.

—the butterfly effect

When they are kids, it seems like a
profession—talking to rocks and
listening for their beauty. For the song
that says that they belong together. They
pick up—

the shiny one,
the round one,
the flat one,
the pretty one.

They store them
in boxes,
in bags,
in pockets.

(Don't worry;
they are very clean
after being laundered.)

But what you will miss, unless
you pay attention is this:

There is always the possibility that
we can treasure what is in our pockets,
rather than the thing we have yet to attain.

There is the knowledge of the earth beneath
all of us that a plain sparkly rock can give.
It is the hurtling round rock on which we
race around the universe.

There is the sense of beauty all around, but
also choosing to experience it, to seize it and
savor it. You could do worse than a practical,
ongoing yes.

This community will not begrudge you any
reminder of your individual, our shared strength.
Carry it with you everywhere. Be ready to
share it; you know where you can get more.

—*A Rock in Our Pocket*

It is a truth, though it may not always
feel like one, that you are worth more
than the things that you do. That your being
a worthy human being lives in a
different domain than all of your failures,
but also the collected sum of your successes.

Combining your worth with your results
is something like using the sheet music for
Beethoven's Fifth Symphony to make an
apple pie or build a dog house. There is no
way for the question to resolve in a final
answer.

By virtue of being alive, you matter, and
you cannot be more deserving of dignity,
of respect, of love. Sometimes people make
mistakes, but even that cannot change that
you are meant to be festooned with celebration
of your humanity.

If your progress is slow, your movements small,
remember that you don't have to compete for
compassion. You don't have to compare what you
can observe of another's life to make sure that you
measure up. You are definitely yourself.

What is slow is also valuable. Some of the oldest
seeds ever sprouted are narrow-leafed campion
that grew, even though the seeds were thirty-two

thousand

years old, more or less. They had to survive to be able
to bloom. Encased in ice, thawed, and brought to life.

The most important thing is that you make it.
No matter how imperceptible the movement, how
long it takes to reach the best version of who you
mean to be. You are irreplaceable. You are meant to live.

—*The Life Slow and Precious*

The day we are in is not unprecedented entirely.
America has been unjust before, has ignored both
its laws and what higher law the soul can sense—
that each person is a human and as a human,
it turns out that their life and their body belongs
expressly to them.

That is, if they come for my queer body, I will resist.
For totalitarianism to thrive, there must be
an enemy created. We have watched
as queers, as trans and non-binary folk,
and our Black and brown neighbors, workers, have been
made into the wanted poster [unwanted faces].

The mild reaction of many people I would have trusted
communicates clearly that they see no danger and that
I should wait until it gets bad. America, your sickness
makes me sit and weep. We will rise. Of course, but

Will it be enough? The babies are already in cages.
Is that not your alarm? Are you not awake? Bolt upright?
Your trans kin are stuck struggling to navigate systems
that actively exert the power to define them out of
existence, to deny travel documents, health care.
America, is this freedom? Who is free?

All is not lost. But some is gone. The part of society
that could assume that being decent was enough of
an expectation to keep us civil is discovering that
disconnected from values, any practice can be

destructive. The time to politely look away, as
though cruelty is merely somewhat impolite,
expired some time back. We must get free.
Do something to be faithful. Do something to
interrupt evil. Do not wait. Do it now. The time
we have left for collecting courage and dealing
in compassion is not unlimited. But this is still your
day. Move into it in your power and your love.

—*America, is this freedom?*

El valor y la dignidad de cada
persona
Imagina que llegó el día
en que dejamos de tasar a
las personas como si fueran
casas o montones de recursos.

The worth and dignity of every
person.

Imagine that the day arrived
in which we left behind valua-
tions of people as though they
were houses or bundles of
resources.

Personas siempre poseídas
del conocimiento de que
siempre son alguien, nunca
nadie.

Persons always possessed
of the knowledge that they
are always somebody, never
nobody.

De que el color de la piel,
las fuentes del lenguaje, la
distancia del hogar no define
a quién merece la pena de
nuestro apoyo, nuestro cariño

82

y el sentido de pertenecer
a esta comunidad, en este
momento, con estas posibili-
dades.

That skin color, sources of
language, or distance from
home doesn't define who
is worthy of our support,
our caring, and the sense of
belonging in this community,
in this moment, with these
possibilities.

Este momento se siente peli-
groso. Hay algo que se resiste
a todas las dignidades que
no son las de la gente blanca,
algo que lastima y pone en
riesgo la vida de los demás.

This moment feels danger-
ous. There is something that
resists all the dignities that
are not those of white folks,
damaging, risking the rest of
the lives.

¿Cómo responderemos?

¿Cuál es la respuesta? ¿Qué
inspira el Primer Principio?

How shall we respond? What
is there for an answer? What
does the First Principle itself
inspire?

Levantémonos en contra de
todo poder injusto, en contra
del ejercicio del poder sin
límite ni ética.

Let us rise against every unjust
power, against the exercise of
power without limits or ethics.

Es hora de imaginar un
día diferente, una conexión
innegable con el universo
entero. Libertad en abundan-
cia y paz en cada corazón.

It's time to imagine a different
day, an undeniable connection
to the entire universe. Free-
dom in abundance and peace
in every heart.

—*Siete principios de unitario universalista, bueno, más el primero*

I need you to know
that there is nothing
wrong with you, if you
find the world congealed
and unwieldy. You were
never meant to serve money,
to give loyalty to unprincipled
power, to spend your joy
frantically soothing yourself
in order to tend wounds
of being constantly
dehumanized.
I need you
to know that your sense
of injury and anger is not
overdeveloped. You are meant
for love and beauty. You belong
where you are known and
where your future is not just a
resource, but a promise, which
you begin to fulfill by being
unmistakably, irrevocably
yourself.

—*You are not wrong*

I confess that I have skipped to the back
of the back of the book. I really wanted to know what
or who or how the story went. I told myself that if I
still wanted to read the rest, then it must be good.
But that only works for paperback books.
Life is a little less linear. And still wanting to know
how the journey will go, I am willing to dance with
the suspense. What will become of a failure? What
can be built with an honest mistake? Keep paying
attention. Keep dreaming and supposing that more
is possible. We don't yet know the ending. And if
you are tired, then it must be time to rest. Staying
curious is like a muscle. We flex—reaching for what
we don't yet know. And relax—leaving space for what
is yet to come.

—*Stretch*

My colleague and friend, Alex Haider-Winnett, a ministerial intern, shared a photo with me recently. It showed the last page of a sermon of theirs that they were analyzing.

The last few lines read, "Reach out and save love. And know that love will reach out and save you back.

And now, let us pray."

Then, in tall red letters, written with a marker, Alex adds, "Ahh . . . the old 'not-an-ending' ending. . . . How many times can I say, 'We're all in this together'? I feel that I was struggling not to end on a bummer, to offer some sense of hope. But I am not sure that this is right now."

If you're a person charged with giving a good word in a congregation or a community context, if you minister at the very same time that your heart is broken, you may relate to Alex's struggle.

Hope is the thing inside you that says yes in the face of every no. The thing that will not give up is not a magical answer. We find ourselves in a time that is equal parts cruelty and confusion. There are even times when the confusion is a tool of systems of oppression. It is control, by which people who resist can be pressed to indecision. Or rather, indecision can distract good people from a series of right acts meant to amount to organized resistance.

This means that if you bring a good word rooted in the will of your people it will be the one they are waiting for. This is true even if you cannot tie it up in a pretty bow with an optimistic conclusion. Optimism is more than just being in a good mood, regardless of the turn toward fascism that we see all around us.

There aren't infinite ways to say that we're in this together; that's the truth. Yet, we retain our loyalty to reality and truth. Our ongoing acknowledgment that each of us is somebody means that we don't need many finely crafted ways to say that in an uncertain and confusing world, the certainty we offer isn't that we have all the right answers or even all the right actions. Rather, we present the certainty that no matter what happens, we aim to move forward together. We need to get out of our own way as we give up the tools of the systems of oppression and control that we are a part of. We must choose to give up racism and classism, transphobia and homophobia, sexism, ableism, and other forms of dehumanization.

Our hope is not indefinite. It does not come magically from inside each of us, nor does it exist for ourselves alone. Hope is a practice that we create. Just as mastering physical skills takes a lot of training and practice, mastering communal hope requires that we stay at it and do the actions that will bring about new states of being and new futures. "We are in this together" means that we choose each other, over and over, as sources and communities of hope. Maybe we will repeat it often. Changing our reality often takes more than one try. We are in this together, thank goodness.

—*When There Is No Happy Ending*